It's Game Time!

by
Katherine Scraper

Carson-Dellosa Publishing Company, Inc.
Greensboro, North Carolina

Dedication
to my sister and favorite early childhood educator,
Susan "Library Lady" Bryant

Credits:
Editor: Ashley Futrell
Layout Design: Mark Conrad
Inside Illustrations: Janet Armbrust
Cover Design: Peggy Jackson
Cover Illustrations: Dan Sharp

Printed in the USA • All rights reserved.   ISBN 1-59441-101-8

Table of Contents

Skills for each activity are denoted by the following icons:

Icon	Skill	Examples
	Social	sharing taking turns cooperating
	Memory	remembering repeating imitating
	Oral Language	naming chanting describing
	Fine Motor	holding sorting drawing
	Gross Motor	throwing hopping skipping

Introduction

Why play games with early childhood learners?

* Games reinforce social skills, such as saying "Please" and "Thank you," sharing, taking turns, cooperating, shaking hands, and encouraging each other.
* Games develop listening and memory skills as children learn to follow instructions, respond to cues, and follow multistep processes.
* Games improve oral language development as children ask and answer questions and interact with each other while engaging in structured activities.
* Games provide opportunities for children to develop fine motor and gross motor coordination and learn directional terms as they manipulate objects and move around an area.
* Games afford the ideal context in which to teach, reinforce, and practice new concepts.
* Games are play, and play is a child's work.

It's Game Time! includes over 100 games that are based on a variety of early childhood concepts. Each game includes easy-to-follow preparation instructions and step-by-step activity directions. And, many of the games can be adapted for whole-group, small-group, or individual play. *Caution:* Some games require a variety of small objects and manipulatives. Remember that small pieces may present a choking hazard for young children and select manipulatives and game pieces according to students' needs.

Are you ready? Are you set? Then, let's go! It's game time!

Adaptable Games

Many of the games in *It's Game Time!* can be adapted to fit a variety of early childhood themes. For your convenience, some simple variations are listed in this chapter.

Pop-Up Letters

Ready: Choose several familiar letters and write each one on a separate index card. Make two cards for each letter. You should have enough cards for each student to receive one card.

Set: Have students sit on the floor in a circle. Give each student a letter card.

Go: Randomly call on two students. These two students should announce the letters that are on their cards. If the letters match, the players should "pop up" (jump) and remain standing. If the letters do not match, the students should remain seated. Continue until all of the players are standing. Now, have students pass their cards to the left, sit down, and play again.

Variations:

Pop-Up Colors

Program the cards with familiar color swatches. Make two cards for each color. Or, you may want to write the color words in color, depending on students' developmental levels. For example, you could write the word *blue* with a blue marker.

Pop-Up Numbers

Program the cards with familiar numbers, such as 1 through 10. Make two cards for each number.

Pop-Up Shapes

Program the cards with drawings of familiar shapes, such as circles, squares, rectangles, or triangles. Make two cards for each shape.

Pop-Up Clocks

Reproduce the Blank Clock Cards (page 68) on sturdy paper or card stock. Draw hands on the clocks to represent familiar times to the hour. Make two cards for each time.

Pop-Up Words

Program the cards with illustrated familiar words for students to match. Make two cards for each word. You may want to create several sets of cards to accommodate a variety of categories, such as classroom items, pets, favorite foods, etc.

Alphabet!

Ready: Program index cards by writing a familiar letter on each card. Make at least two cards for each letter.

Set: Have one student be the Alphabet Captain. Have other players sit in a large circle around the Alphabet Captain, either in chairs or on the floor. Give each child in the circle a letter card.

Go: The Alphabet Captain should call out a letter. All of the students with that letter card should jump up and trade places while the Alphabet Captain tries to sit in one of the empty seats. The child left standing becomes the Alphabet Captain for the next round. The Alphabet Captain also has the option of calling out, "Alphabet!" instead of saying a letter. When this happens, all of the players in the room should try to switch seats. Again, the child left standing without a seat will become the Alphabet Captain for the next round.

Variations:

Rainbow!

Program the cards with familiar color swatches. Make at least two cards for each color. Or, you may want to write the color words in color, depending on students' developmental levels. In this version of the game, the Color Captain has the option of calling out, "Rainbow!"

Numbers!

Program the cards with familiar numbers, such as 1 through 10. Make at least two cards for each number. In this version of the game, the Number Captain has the option of calling out, "Numbers!"

Shapes!

Program the cards with drawings of familiar shapes, such as circles, squares, triangles, and rectangles. Make at least two cards for each shape. In this version of the game, the Shape Captain has the option of calling out, "Shapes!"

Ticktock Time!

Reproduce the Blank Clock Cards (page 68) on sturdy paper or card stock. Draw hands on the clocks to represent familiar times to the hour. Make at least two cards for each time. In this version of the game, the Time Captain has the option of calling out, "Ticktock Time!"

Letter Bingo

Ready: Make enough copies of the Bingo Board (page 8) for each student to have his own board. Program each board with a variety of familiar letters. Prepare a set of small cards, one card for each letter that you used on the bingo boards. Laminate all of the boards and cards for durability. Prepare space markers for each child by filling a snack-sized, resealable, plastic bag with cereal or small manipulatives.

Set: Give each child a game board and a bag of space markers. Shuffle the small cards.

Go: Have each student place one marker on the *Free* space. Select a letter card and show it to the children as you name the letter. Each student who has that letter on his board should cover it with a space marker. If the letter appears on a student's board more than once, he should only cover it one time. The first student to cover a complete row of letters should raise his hand and call out, "Bingo!" (You should decide before playing the game if a "row" includes horizontal, vertical, and/or diagonal lines.) The student who correctly fills a row first is the winner for that round, and if you choose to use cereal as space markers, everyone can celebrate together by eating the cereal from his game board. Continue playing as time (and cereal) allows. (*Caution:* Before completing any food activity, ask parental permission and inquire about students' food allergies and religious or other preferences.)

Variations:

Color Bingo

Program each board with a variety of familiar color swatches. Or, you may want to write the color words in color, depending on students' developmental levels. Prepare a set of small cards, one card for each color swatch that you used on the boards.

Number Bingo

Program each board with a variety of familiar numbers, such as 1 through 10. Prepare a set of small cards, one card for each number that you used on the boards.

Shape Bingo

Program each board with drawings of familiar shapes, such as circles, squares, triangles, and rectangles. Prepare a set of small cards, one card for each shape that you used on the boards.

Time Bingo

Program each board with drawings of clock faces. Draw hands on the clocks to represent familiar times to the hour. Prepare a set of small cards, one card for each time that you used on the boards.

Bingo Board

Activities found on page 7.

B	I	N	G	O
		FREE		

Alphabet Cheer

Ready: Program index cards by writing a familiar letter on each card. Make several cards for each letter. Prepare extra cards with drawings of stick figures jumping in the air, waving their arms, and cheering, "Yeah!" Or, cut out magazine pictures of children jumping in the air and glue them to the cards.

Set: Shuffle the cards together and place them facedown on your lap.

Go: As you hold up the cards one at a time, students should call out the letter on each card. If a stick figure card is shown, students should jump in the air, wave their arms, and cheer, "Yeah!" Continue until all of the cards are used.

Variations:

Color Cheer

Program the cards with a variety of familiar color swatches. Or, you may want to write the color words in color, depending on students' developmental levels. Make several cards for each color swatch.

Number Cheer

Program the cards with a variety of familiar numbers, such as 1 through 10. Make several cards for each number.

Shape Cheer

Program the cards with drawings of familiar shapes, such as circles, squares, triangles, and rectangles. Make several cards for each shape.

Clock Cheer

Reproduce the Blank Clock Cards (page 68) on sturdy paper or card stock. Draw hands on the clocks to represent familiar times to the hour. Make several clocks for each time.

Word Cheer

Program the cards with illustrated familiar words for students to match. You may want to create several sets of word cards to accommodate a variety of categories, such as classroom items, pets, favorite foods, etc. Make several cards for each illustrated word.

Musical Letter Chairs

Ready: Set up a circle of chairs, including one chair for each child in the class. The chairs should face the outer edge of the circle. Using large index cards or sturdy card stock, label each chair with a familiar letter. Prepare a set of small cards, one card for each letter that you used to label the chairs. Select upbeat music that can be easily started and stopped.

Set: Give each child a small letter card. Tell the children to make a circle around the chairs.

Go: When you start the music, the players should march around the chairs. When you stop the music, each child should quickly (but carefully!) find the labeled chair that matches his letter card and sit in it. When all of the children have found their seats, each student should trade cards with a classmate and start the game again.

Variations:

Musical Color Chairs

Label each chair with a familiar color swatch. Or, you may want to write the color words in color, depending on students' developmental levels. Make a matching set of small cards for the color swatches.

Musical Number Chairs

Label each chair with a familiar number, such as 1 through 10. Make a matching set of small cards for the numbers.

Musical Shape Chairs

Label each chair with a drawing of a familiar shape, such as a circle, square, triangle, or rectangle. Make a matching set of small cards for the shapes.

Musical Word Chairs

Label each chair with an illustrated familiar word. You may want to create several sets of word cards to accommodate a variety of categories, such as classroom items, pets, favorite foods, etc. Make a matching set of small cards for the illustrated words.

Letter Guessing Game  ....

Ready: Program index cards by writing a familiar letter on each card. Draw a smiley face on a smaller card.

Set: Place the letter cards in a pocket chart, line them in a row on the board ledge, or attach them to a bulletin board with pushpins. Hide the smiley face card behind one of the larger letter cards.

Go: Randomly call on students one at a time. When a student is selected, she should come to the front of the classroom and point to and name a letter card. You should then help her remove the letter card to see if the smiley face is behind it. Continue randomly calling on students to guess letters until the smiley face is found. When a student finds the smiley face, instruct the rest of the class to cover their eyes while the student hides the smiley face behind a different letter. Play again.

Variations:

Color Guessing Game
Program the cards with familiar color swatches. Or, you may want to write the color words in color, depending on students' developmental levels.

Number Guessing Game
Program the cards with familiar numbers, such as 1 through 10.

Shape Guessing Game
Program the cards with drawings of familiar shapes, such as circles, squares, triangles, and rectangles.

Time Guessing Game
Reproduce the Blank Clock Cards (page 68) on sturdy paper or card stock. Draw hands on the clocks to represent familiar times to the hour. Depending on students' developmental levels, you may want to write the corresponding digital times below each clock face.

Word Guessing Game
Program the cards with illustrated familiar words. You may want to create several sets of word cards to accommodate a variety of categories, such as classroom items, pets, favorite foods, etc.

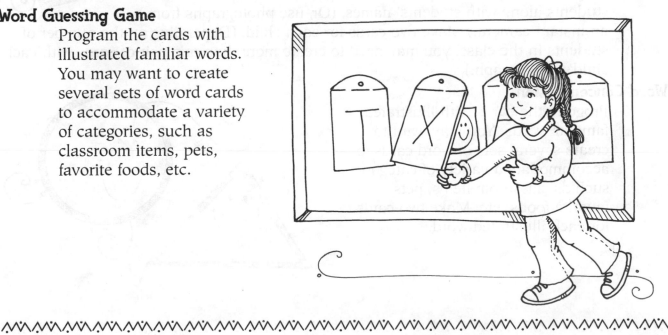

Letter Concentration

Ready: Program index cards by writing a familiar letter on each card. Make two cards for each letter. You will need enough sets of index cards to supply each pair of children with three to five matching pairs of cards.

Set: Divide students into pairs. Give each pair of children three to five matching pairs of cards. Students should mix the cards and lay them facedown in equal rows.

Go: Each player takes a turn flipping over any two cards. He should name the letters on the two cards. If the cards match, the student gets to keep that pair. If they do not match, they are placed facedown in the same spots, and the other player takes her turn. The game ends when all of the cards have been matched. Have students repeat the game after reshuffling the cards or after trading cards with another pair of students.

Variations:

Color Concentration

Program the cards with familiar color swatches. Or, you may want to write the color words in color, depending on students' developmental levels. Make two cards for each color swatch.

Number Concentration

Program the cards with familiar numbers, such as 1 through 10. Make two cards for each number.

Shape Concentration

Program the cards with drawings of familiar shapes, such as circles, squares, triangles, and rectangles. Make two cards for each shape.

Name Concentration

Program the cards with printouts of digital photographs of students along with students' names. (Or, use photographs from an instant camera.) Make two cards for each child. (Depending on the number of students in the class, you may need to create more than one pair of cards with each child's photograph.)

Word Concentration

Program the cards with illustrated familiar words. You may want to create several sets of word cards to accommodate a variety of categories, such as classroom items, pets, favorite foods, etc. Make two cards for each illustrated word.

Letter Dominoes ♡ ? ✋ ....

Ready: Make several copies of the Domino Patterns (page 14) on sturdy card stock. Cut apart the dominoes along the thin, dashed lines and program them with a variety of familiar letters, using a different letter on each half of each domino. Use all of the letters twice so that each letter will have a match. Consider laminating the dominoes for durability.

Set: This game requires at least two players. Instruct players to mix the dominoes and place them facedown on a table.

Go: Each player should select four dominoes. The first player should begin by placing a domino faceup on the table. If the next player has a domino that matches one side of the first player's domino, she should place the matching letters next to each other. If she does not have a matching domino, she should draw from the pile until she draws a domino that has a matching letter. The game continues until one player has used all of his dominoes. The dominoes may then be placed facedown and mixed again for another round.

Variations:

Color Dominoes

Program the dominoes with familiar color swatches, using a different color swatch on each half of each domino. Use all of the color swatches twice so that each color will have a match. Or, write the color words in color, depending on students' developmental levels.

Counting Dots Dominoes

Program the dominoes with dots, using a different number of dots on each half of each domino. (Use dots to represent familiar numbers, such as 1 through 10.) Use all of the dot combinations twice so that each one will have a match.

Shape Dominoes

Program the dominoes with drawings of familiar shapes, such as circles, squares, triangles, and rectangles, using a different shape on each half of each domino. Use all of the shapes twice so that each shape will have a match.

Domino Patterns

Activities found on page 13.

CD-104045 *It's Game Time!*

Color Games

Button Relay

Ready: Collect a supply of buttons in three or four familiar colors. For each button color, copy one Button Pattern (page 16) on paper of the same color. You may want to laminate the paper buttons for durability. Attach each paper button to a container.

Set: Divide the buttons evenly into two bowls. Make sure there is an assortment of colors in each bowl. Line the labeled containers on a table at one end of the room. At the other end of the room, place another table with the two bowls of assorted buttons. Divide students into two teams. Have each team form a single file line on one side of the table with the two bowls of buttons.

Go: The first child on each team should grab a small handful of buttons from the team's bowl, run (hop, skip, etc.) to the containers, and sort the buttons by color. (You should stand by the sorting table to make sure that colors are sorted correctly and offer assistance if needed.) When the buttons are sorted successfully, the player should run (hop, skip, etc.) back to the starting line to tag the next player on her team. The next player should then repeat the process, continuing until each student has had a turn or the buttons are gone. The first team to finish is the winner. Replace the buttons in the bowls and play again.

Color Clues

Ready: Collect a sheet of drawing paper and a set of crayons or markers for each player. Compose a variety of word rhymes about familiar colors. Write each rhyme on an index card. Some sample rhymes include *red bed, blue shoe, yellow fellow, black sack, brown crown, green bean, pink sink, white kite, tan van,* etc.

Set: Seat students at tables or on the floor with their drawing paper and crayons.

Go: Select a card and read the rhyme to yourself (not aloud). Then, give a clue, such as, "It rhymes with *red*, and you sleep in it." Players should raise their hands if they think they know the answer. Call on a student to guess the answer. When the correct answer is given, provide time for students to draw pictures of the answer, using the appropriate color. Repeat with the other game cards.

Variation: For a challenge, have students wait to guess the answer to the riddle until after they have taken time to draw. When everyone is finished drawing, ask for volunteers to guess the answer.

Button Patterns

Activity found on page 15.

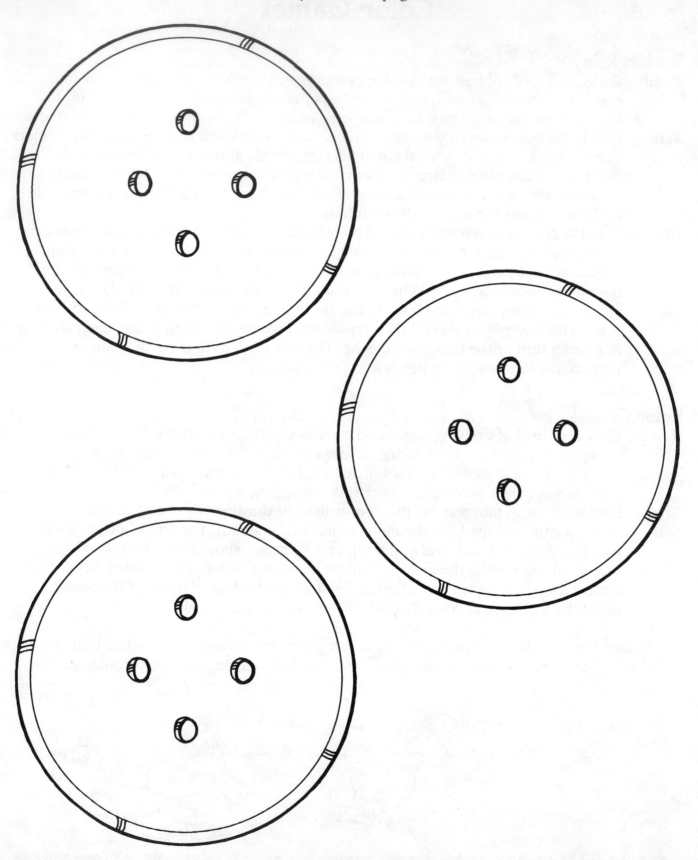

ᐯᐯᐯᐯᐯᐯᐯᐯᐯᐯᐯᐯᐯᐯᐯᐯᐯᐯᐯᐯᐯᐯᐯᐯᐯᐯᐯ

The Color of a Tomato ....

Ready: Prepare a set of construction paper squares in familiar colors, such as red, yellow, orange, green, blue, purple, black, white, and brown. Each player will need her own set of these cards.

Set: Seat children at tables or on the floor with their color cards spread in front of them.

Go: Call out a clue, such as, "Show me the color of a tomato." Each student should look through her paper squares, choose the appropriate color, and hold it up. When everyone has agreed, give a cheer for the color, such as, "Red, red, we love red!" Repeat with other color clues.

Clothing Colors ....

Ready: Program index cards with familiar color swatches. Make a second set of cards by copying and cutting apart the Clothing Cards (page 18). Do not color the clothing cards; they need to be black-and-white drawings. You may want to laminate the cards for durability.

Set: Place the two sets of cards into separate containers. Have students stand in a circle.

Go: Draw a card from each container and show the cards to students. Announce what is on each card. For example, you might say, "Red socks." In this case, players who are wearing red socks should sit down. Continue drawing cards and calling out clothing items and colors. You may need to shuffle the cards and continue calling out items if all of the students have not been seated. The last student standing is the winner. When the round is over, have all of the children stand and play again.

Variation: Instead of having students simply sit down when an item of their clothing is chosen, have them perform three jumping jacks, hop like a frog, act like a monkey, or do some other silly stunt before sitting.

ᐯᐯᐯᐯᐯᐯᐯᐯᐯᐯᐯᐯᐯᐯᐯᐯᐯᐯᐯᐯᐯᐯᐯᐯᐯᐯᐯ

Clothing Cards

Activity found on page 17.

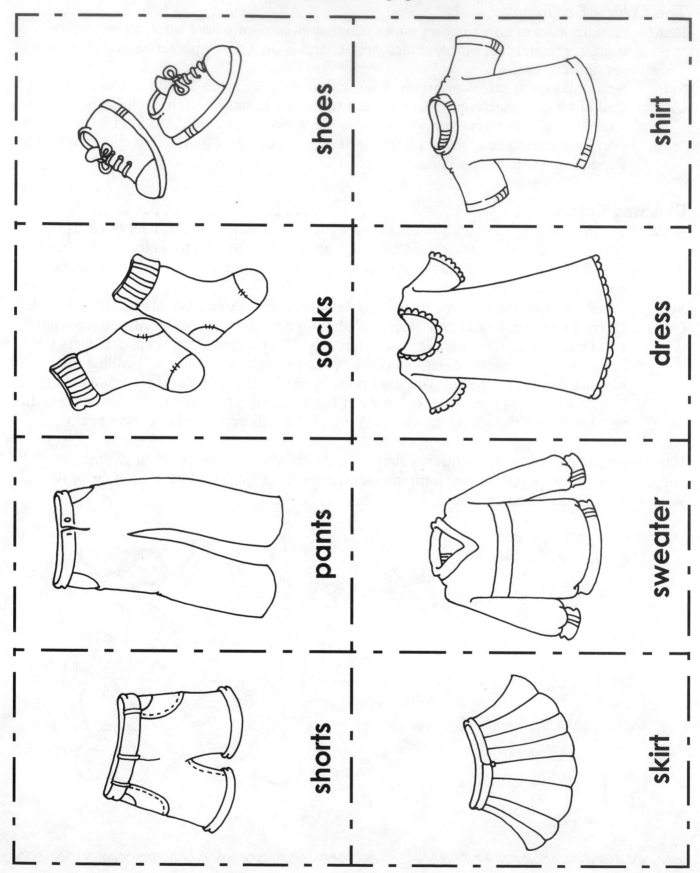

shoes

shirt

socks

dress

pants

sweater

shorts

skirt

My Three Blocks

Ready: Gather a set of blocks for each student. Each student's set should include three blocks in three different familiar colors, such as red, yellow, and blue. For convenience, place each set in a small bag.

Set: Have students sit cross-legged in a circle on the floor. Each child should place her three blocks in front of her.

Go: Call out instructions, such as, "Place the red block on top of the yellow block and the blue block on top of the red block," or "Place the yellow block on the left, the blue block in the middle, and the red block on the right," etc. After each set of instructions, give students time to arrange their blocks. You may want to model the correct placement with your own set of blocks, depending on students' developmental levels. After students are all in agreement about the correct arrangement of the blocks, give the next set of instructions.

Beach Ball Colors

Ready: Acquire a striped beach ball with traditional colors or decorate a plain beach ball with stripes of different colors.

Set: Arrange students in a large circle.

Go: Call out a child's name as you toss the beach ball to her and say, "Left thumb!" or "Right thumb!" as the ball is in the air. The child should catch the ball and say the name of the color that the thumb is touching. She then tosses the ball and calls on another child to continue the game.

ᴧᴧᴧᴧᴧᴧᴧᴧᴧᴧᴧᴧᴧᴧᴧᴧᴧᴧᴧᴧᴧᴧᴧᴧᴧᴧᴧᴧᴧᴧᴧᴧᴧᴧᴧᴧᴧᴧᴧ

Ickety, Ackety

Ready: Program index cards with familiar color swatches.

Set: When it is time to have students line up to leave the classroom, have them gather together and sit on the floor.

Go: Select and display one of the color cards. Chant together:

Ickety, Ackety, (Ellow),
Line up now if you're wearing (yellow)!

Change the nonsense word at the end of the first line to rhyme with the various colors. For example, you might say, "Ooo" for blue, "Een" for green, "Ack" for black, "Ed" for red, "Urple" for purple, etc. Continue displaying cards and saying the rhyme until all of the children are in line.

Color Ring Toss

Ready: Gather several clear, plastic, two-liter bottles. Empty and clean the bottles and remove their labels so that the contents will be easily viewable. You will need enough bottles for each familiar color you wish to include in the game. Fill each bottle with water and add a different color of food coloring to each bottle. Seal the bottles tightly. If you wish, label each bottle with the color word written on a self-stick label. Acquire several embroidery hoops. Make a set of cards to match the selected colors by placing color swatches on index cards.

Set: Place the bottles in a row on the floor with plenty of space between the bottles. Mix up the color cards and place them facedown.

Go: Each child should take a turn drawing a card and attempting to toss a hoop over the bottle with the matching color. Keep a tally of successful throws for the whole class. After everyone has taken a turn, retrieve the hoops and repeat the game. Compare the scores from round to round to see how students' accuracy is improving as a group.

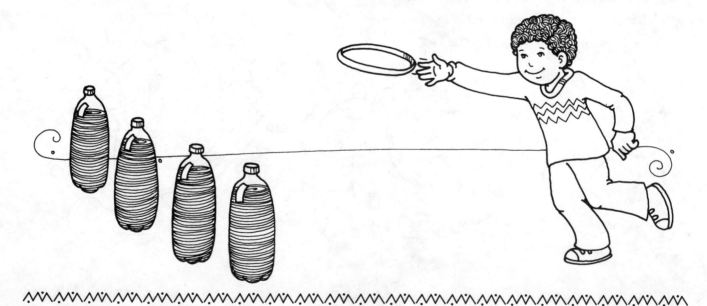

ᴧᴧᴧᴧᴧᴧᴧᴧᴧᴧᴧᴧᴧᴧᴧᴧᴧᴧᴧᴧᴧᴧᴧᴧᴧᴧᴧᴧᴧᴧᴧᴧᴧᴧᴧᴧᴧᴧᴧ

NVVVVVVVVVVVVVVVVVVVVVVVVVVVVVVVV

Graph-A-Pattern

Ready: Make enough copies of the Graph Paper (page 22) for each student to have his own sheet. Collect a variety of colorful connecting cubes and crayons in the same colors. Each child will need his own set of crayons.

Set: Give each student a set of crayons and a sheet of graph paper. Arrange the connecting cubes into a color pattern, such as blue-blue-red-yellow.

Go: Each player should duplicate the pattern on the graph paper by coloring one square for each cube. Then, he should fill in the rest of the row on the graph paper in the same pattern. When students have finished coloring their patterns, call on a student to make a new connecting cube pattern for classmates to duplicate. Continue the game until each child has had a turn to create a new pattern.

Fishing

Ready: Copy the Fish Patterns (page 23) on an assortment of colorful paper or card stock. You will need approximately six fish for each color. Cut out the fish and laminate them for durability. Gather enough containers for each color and label them by attaching a different color fish to each one. Prepare a "fishing pole" by attaching a length of string to a yardstick (meterstick). Attach a magnet to serve as the "hook" on the end of the "fishing line."

Set: Affix paper clips to the mouths of the fish patterns and place them in a large tub.

Go: Each player should take a turn using the fishing pole to "catch" a fish. When a player "reels in" a fish, she should name the fish's color and place it in the correct container. When all of the fish have been caught, return them to the tub and start over.

Variation: To make the game more challenging, call out a particular color fish for each student to catch.

NVVVVVVVVVVVVVVVVVVVVVVVVVVVVVVVV

Graph Paper

Activity found on page 21.

CD-104045 *It's Game Time!*

Fish Patterns

Activity found on page 21.

CD-104045 *It's Game Time!*

Jumping Beans

Ready: Paint dried lima beans in a variety of familiar colors and let them dry. Or, copy the Bean Patterns (page 25) on colorful card stock. Cut out the bean shapes and laminate them for durability. You should make or paint at least five beans for each color.

Set: Place the painted beans (or bean cutouts) in a large bowl. Choose one student to be the Jumping Bean.

Go: Instruct all of the children to cover their eyes while the Jumping Bean secretly selects a bean from the bowl. After he looks at the color, he should give you the bean to hide it from view and keep the color a secret. Now, instruct the rest of the class to uncover their eyes. The Jumping Bean should now begin hopping and chanting:

> *I'm a jumping bean; see me hop.*
> *Guess my color and then I'll stop!*

The other children in the class should take turns guessing different colors. When the correct color is named, the Jumping Bean should stop jumping, retrieve the bean from you, and show it to the class. The player who correctly guesses the color becomes the next Jumping Bean, and the game continues.

Bean Patterns

Activity found on page 24.

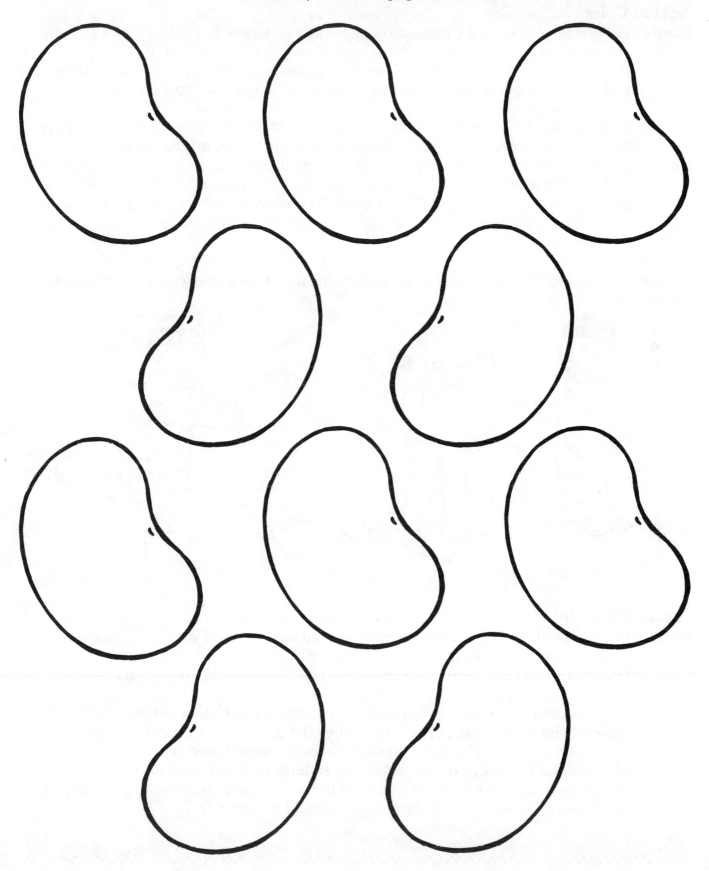

∿∿∿∿∿∿∿∿∿∿∿∿∿∿∿∿∿∿∿∿∿∿∿∿∿∿

Action Colors ♡ ? 👟 . . . .

Ready: Provide large sheets of construction paper in a variety of familiar colors. Laminate the paper for durability. Each child in the class will need her own piece of paper. If, for example, there are 16 students in the class but they only know eight colors, you can include two pieces of paper for each color and have students perform the activities in pairs.

Set: Tape the sheets of paper randomly on the floor. Make sure there is plenty of space between the pieces. Assemble the students in a circle around the paper.

Go: Call out a student's name and give him an instruction, such as, "Walk backward to blue," "Hop to red," "Crab walk to yellow," "Gallop to green," or "Skip to orange." After a player performs his action, he should remain standing in that spot while his classmates take their turns. After each child has had a turn, have students return to the circle and start again.

Variation: Play music while students are performing the actions to encourage a variety of movement.

Pattern Match ♡ ? 👒 . . . .

Ready: Provide chenille craft sticks and several small containers of wooden beads in a variety of familiar colors.

Set: Divide students into pairs. Give each pair two chenille craft sticks and a small container of beads.

Go: One student in each pair should string a pattern of beads on a chenille craft stick, such as yellow, red, blue, yellow, red, blue. The other student should copy the pattern on the other chenille craft stick. Students should then hold the two chenille craft sticks side-by-side to check that the patterns match. If they do not match, the students should work together to correct the second pattern. Once they match, the beads can be removed, and the students should reverse roles.

∿∿∿∿∿∿∿∿∿∿∿∿∿∿∿∿∿∿∿∿∿∿∿∿∿∿

Letter and Word Games

Hop to It!

Ready: Program familiar letters on large pieces of sturdy card stock. Each letter card should be approximately 1' x 1' (30.5 cm x 30.5 cm). Make a matching set of small cards, each approximately 3" x 3" (7.5 cm x 7.5 cm). Laminate the cards for durability.

Set: Spread the large cards randomly on the floor and tape them securely in place. Place the small cards in a bag (or bowl).

Go: Students should take turns selecting a small card from the bag and hopping to the matching large card on the floor. When the student reaches the matching floor card, she should stand on it while other students take their turns. Continue playing until each child has had a turn. Then, collect the small cards and start again. To make the game more challenging, write lowercase letters on the small cards and matching uppercase letters on the large floor cards.

Variation: When a player reaches the floor card, he should say a word or make a sound that starts with his letter.

Extension: Play different types of music to encourage various kinds of movement when students are traveling to their letters. For example, you might choose a song with a fast tempo and instruct children to hop like speedy bunnies to their letters. Or, you might choose a slow, laboring song and instruct children to walk like giant elephants to their letters.

Alphabet Search

Ready: Gather a collection of familiar magnetic or foam letters. Include as many pieces as possible for each letter. Do not include the entire alphabet until students are able to easily recognize all of the letters. Place the letters in a large tub or bucket. Next, add dried pasta, beans, popcorn kernels, or rice and mix well. Write each letter that you included on a large index card. Laminate the cards for durability.

Set: Place the tub on the floor and spread the letter cards nearby.

Go: Each student should take a turn digging in the tub with her hands until she locates a letter and place it on or near the matching letter card. Continue until all of the letters have been located and sorted. (*Caution:* Small pieces may present a choking hazard for young children.)

Reach and Match

Ready: Cut a hole in the lid of a box. The hole should be just large enough for a child to reach inside the box without seeing its contents. Choose an assortment of letters that the class is currently studying. Fill the box with small items that have names beginning with the letters. Write each letter on an index card.

Set: Place the letter cards on a table around the box. Have students sit in a circle around the table.

Go: Each player should take a turn reaching into the box, grabbing an object, naming it, and placing it on or near the matching letter card. The other players should agree or disagree with the match by showing a "thumbs-up" or "thumbs-down." You or a volunteer should be prepared to assist, as needed, if children are having difficulty agreeing about the match.

What Does It Say?

Ready: Display familiar magnetic letters on a cookie sheet or place felt letters on a felt board. Write each letter on an index card.

Set: This game requires two players. Give one player the cookie sheet or felt board with the letters attached to it. The other player will need access to the stack of letter cards.

Go: One player should draw a letter card from the stack without letting the other player see it. While the second player continues to avert her eyes, the first player should use his finger to slowly trace the letter on the other child's palm. The second child should try to guess which letter was traced on her palm by pointing to the letter on the cookie sheet or felt board. If she guesses incorrectly, the first player should trace the letter again. When she guesses correctly, both students should name the letter aloud. After the first player has traced three letters for the second player, players should switch roles. (You may want to review proper letter formation with students in order to avoid frustration.)

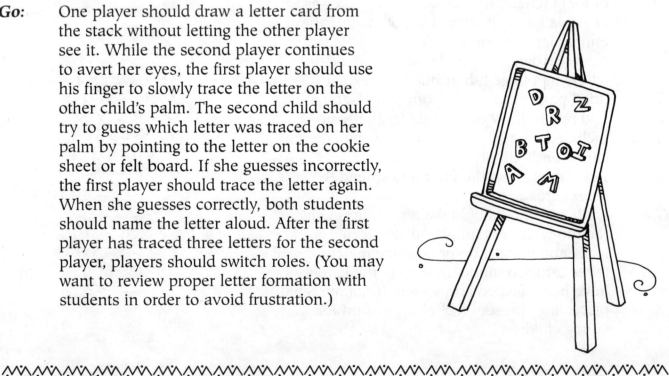

Alphabet Soup

Ready: Gather a collection of familiar magnetic or foam letters. Include as many pieces as possible for each letter. Do not include the entire alphabet until students are able to easily recognize all of the letters. Place the letters into a cooking pot. Provide a ladle. Collect 26 half-pint milk cartons. Open the tops of the cartons completely so that students can reach into them. Clean and dry the cartons. Label each carton with an uppercase and lowercase letter, from Aa to Zz, then place all of the cartons in a row in alphabetical order. You may want to paper clip or staple the cartons together.

Set: Place the pot of letters, the ladle, and the labeled milk cartons on a table.

Go: Each student should take a turn stirring the "alphabet soup" and dipping out one letter with the ladle. He should then name the letter and place it into the appropriate milk carton. Continue until all of the letters are used and each student has had at least one turn to play.

Magnetic Match

Ready: Gather a variety of small pictures. The pictured items should have names beginning or ending with familiar letters. Search magazines, newspapers, and the Internet to find a wide variety of pictures. Glue each picture to an index card. On the back of each card, write the word that names the picture. Laminate the cards for durability. Then, attach a small strip of magnetic tape to the back of each card. Provide a set of magnetic letters.

Set: Provide a metal surface, such as a cookie sheet or the side of a filing cabinet.

Go: Each student should take a turn selecting a magnetic picture card from the stack and putting it on the metal surface. Then, she should match a magnetic letter to the beginning or ending letter of the picture name. She can check her work by looking at the word on the back of the picture card. Continue playing until all of the cards have been used.

Puzzle Rhymes

Ready: Prepare puzzle rhyme cards by writing pairs of consonant-vowel-consonant rhyming words—such as *hop/pop*, *sit/fit*, *hat/cat*, and *sun/fun*—on index cards. Cut each card into two pieces using a jagged pattern so that the two rhyming words will fit together like a puzzle.

Set: Have students stand in a circle and give each child a puzzle piece with a word on it.

Go: Choose one player to read her card. Whoever has the card with the rhyming word on it should call out the word and move to join his rhyme partner. The two players should sit down together and match their puzzle pieces. Continue around the circle until all of the cards are matched. Then, shuffle and play again.

Jingle Words

Ready: Acquire a small jingle bell for each student. If desired, glue each bell to a craft stick to create an easy handle for a student to hold while ringing the bell. Choose a story that includes a familiar word repeated several times, such as "bear" or "stop."

Set: Seat students in a group on the floor with their jingle bells held quietly in their hands.

Go: Tell students that you are going to read them a story, and you want them to listen carefully for a certain word. Whenever they hear the word, they should ring their jingle bells. To practice, say the word and ring the bells together. Finally, read the story. If needed, model ringing your own bell when the word is read.

Syllable Walk

Ready: Prepare a vertical number line for each child in the class. Using a sentence strip, write the numbers 1, 2, 3, and 4 evenly spaced from bottom to top on the strip. Consider laminating for durability. Create word cards by writing various one-, two-, three-, and four-syllable words on index cards. If needed, include simple illustrations to help students recognize the words.

Set: Have students stand in a large circle with their number lines on the floor in front of them. You should also stand in the circle with your own number line.

Go: Select a word card and read the word aloud. Players should repeat the word slowly, stepping on one number for each syllable. When everyone stops, ask, for example, "How many parts are in the word *win-dow*?" (Emphasize the syllables to help them decide.) Students should check where they are standing on their number lines and reply together, "*Win-dow* has two parts." Students should then return to the beginning of their number lines while you select another word card to start the next round of the game.

Line Up

Ready: Write several sentences on sentence strips. Use familiar words in the sentences, such as *I like cats* or *We go to school*. Then, write each word of each sentence on an index card and remember to add a period after the last word of each sentence.

Set: Shuffle the index cards and give one to each player.

Go: Place one sentence strip in a pocket chart or display it on a bulletin board. Have students read the sentence aloud with you as you point to each word. Next, invite children who have any of the words in the sentence to come to the front of the classroom and hold up their cards. The class should then help you arrange the students in order. Read the sentence aloud together. Continue playing until all of the sentences have been formed.

Name Roll

Ready: Print each student's first name in dark letters on a piece of construction paper. Locate a large rubber playground ball.

Set: Have players sit cross-legged in a large circle. You should also join the circle. Give the ball to one student.

Go: One by one, hold up the name cards. Any student who recognizes the name should raise his hand. Call on a student to read the card aloud. Then, the player who has the ball should roll it to the named student. Continue until all players have been called.

Clues

Ready: Prepare a bag or box with a variety of small items in it. The items' names should begin with consonant sounds, but do not select items that have names beginning with digraphs or blends, such as a shell, a thimble, glasses, or a crown.

Set: Seat students on the floor in front of you. Tell them that you have a bag full of items and you want them to guess what is inside. To help them, you are going to give them clues about the items until they guess correctly.

Go: Think of one of the items in the bag and say its beginning sound. Give players a chance to guess what the item may be. If they do not guess correctly, give a clue about where the item might be found. If students still do not guess it, give a clue about the appearance of the item, such as its color or shape. Continue until the item is guessed and then pull it out and put it next to you. Repeat with the next item.

Repeat After Me

Ready: Make a list of three- or four-word instructions for students to follow, such as *Blink your eyes, Touch your toes, Bend your knees, Hold up your arms,* or *Shake your elbows.*

Set: Have players stand in a large circle. Tell them that when you call out an instruction, such as, "Pat your head," they should do the action while repeating the instruction. However, they should change the word "your" to the word "my" ("Pat <u>my</u> head.").

Go: Call out an action from the list. Listen and watch for the correct response, repeating the instruction if needed. Continue calling out instructions and watching students' responses as time allows.

Name Clap

Ready: Post numbers in various places around the room that match the number of syllables in students' names. Write each player's name on a craft stick and place the sticks in a jar or can.

Set: Have students sit in a line at the front of the room.

Go: Select a name stick. Ask that student to stand facing her classmates and hold up her name stick. The rest of the class should clap the syllables while slowly saying the student's name. Have students continue saying the name and clapping until they are sure of the number of syllables in the word. Then, students should point to the correct number hanging on the wall in the room. The featured student should move to sit by that number. Continue until all of the children have been featured, then discuss which group has the most players and which has the least.

33

Tongue Twister Patterns

Ready: Prepare two index cards for each student, one green card that says *Yes* and one red card that says *No*.

Set: Have students sit cross-legged in a large circle. Give each student a set of two cards.

Go: Repeat a word three times, such as, "Bug, bug, bug." Or, use a pattern with the same word twice and one similar word, such as, "Dog, dad, dog," "Five, fish, fish," or "Red, red, rock." Players should repeat the three words and hold up the *Yes* card if all three words are the same or hold up the *No* card if one of the words is different. Repeat with a new word pattern.

Favorites

Ready: Prepare index cards with different "favorite" category names, such as *favorite color, favorite ice cream, favorite book, favorite pet, favorite food,* or *favorite song.*

Set: Have students gather in the center of the room.

Go: Select a card and call out the category. Call on a student to name his favorite thing in that category. Ask if there are other students who have the same favorite. Have that group sit together in one area of the room. Continue calling on players to name their favorite things in the category and group themselves accordingly. Once the entire class is grouped, have them return to the center of the room and choose another card to begin again.

Noisy Noun Charades

Ready: Locate pictures of animals and objects that make sounds, such as a cat, lawn mower, horse, running faucet, and telephone. Glue the pictures to index cards and write the words that name the items below the pictures.

Set: Have students sit in a large circle. Shuffle the cards and place them facedown.

Go: The first player should stand in the center of the circle, draw a card, and secretly look at it. He should then act like the thing featured on the card, including sound effects. The other players should try to guess what word has been selected. Continue until each student has a turn.

Nonsense Rhymes

Ready: Obtain a container and fill it with items that might be found in that type of container. For example, a backpack might hold a pencil, paper, markers, scissors, and a book. A toolbox might contain a hammer, nails, a wrench, a ruler, and pliers. A suitcase might hold a robe, a toothbrush, a shirt, a comb, and socks.

Set: Seat students in a group on the floor. Stand in front of the class where they can all see you. Show the chosen container to students and tell them that they are going to try to guess what is in it by listening to nonsense rhyming words.

Go: One by one, name the items in the container by using a nonsense rhyming word. For example, you might say, "I have a *zencil* in my backpack," or "I have *bissors* in my backpack." Have players try to guess the items. When they guess correctly, place the items on the table for students to see them. Continue until the container is empty. (*Caution:* Some items may not be appropriate for students to handle. Display items for students to view but do not allow them to handle tools or sharp objects.)

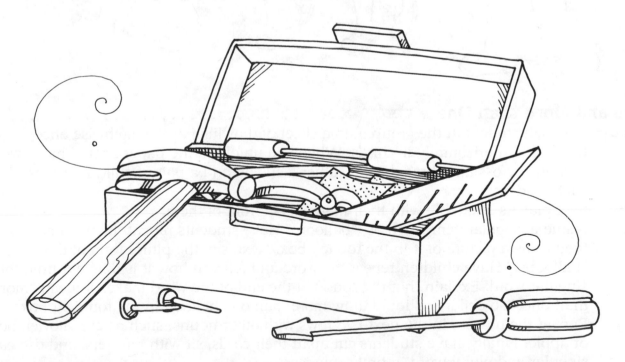

Opcosites ?

Ready: On index cards, write a variety of activity instructions that include words that have opposites, such as *Hold up your hand*, *Take a big step forward*, *Hop to the back of the room*, *Wave your left hand*, or *Make a sad face*.

Set: Have students stand in a large circle. Explain that when you give them a direction, they should do the opposite of what you ask.

Go: Select a card and read the instruction for students to perform. For example, if the instruction says *Wave your left hand*, students should wave their right hands. For the first few rounds, you may need to model how to do an opposite action. As players become more proficient, let them try it on their own.

One and More than One ?

Ready: For each student in the group, fold a sheet of drawing paper lengthwise once, then fold it horizontally in thirds. When you unfold it, the paper should have two sections across and three down. Gather a crayon and a pair of child's scissors for each student.

Set: Seat players at a table with their materials in front of them.

Go: Name a singular item, such as, "balloon." Have students repeat the word and then draw a picture of it in the top left box. Next, say the plural form of the word, "balloons." Have children repeat the word and tell you how it is different from the singular word. Explain that the sound at the end of the word makes it mean "more than one," so children should draw more than one balloon in the top right box. Repeat the process in the next two rows with other nouns, such as cup, flower, book, or apple. Finally, have students cut apart their cards, sit with partners, and use each singular and plural word in oral sentences.

Texture Words

Ready: Collect small objects that are similar in size but not in texture, such as a seashell, yo-yo, and small stuffed animal toy. Find a paper bag large enough to hold all of the items.

Set: Put the objects into the bag and arrange the students in a large circle. You should also join the circle.

Go: One at a time, take each object out of the bag. As you pass each item around the circle, help players think of words that describe it, such as "bumpy," "smooth," or "furry." After all of the items have been examined and discussed, put them back into the bag. Next, name one of the items and call on a student to reach into the bag and find the item without looking. When the correct item is pulled out, the other children should recall as many appropriate describing words as possible. Return the item to the bag and repeat until each child has had a turn.

One, Two, or Three?

Ready: Prepare a bag or box with a variety of small items in it. Items should have names that are one-, two-, or three-syllable words. Prepare a set of three index cards for each student by writing the numbers 1, 2, and 3 on cards.

Set: Have students sit cross-legged in a circle or around a small table with their cards spread in front of them.

Go: Select an item and show it to the class. Ask players to name the object. Together, repeat the word aloud and clap the syllables. Each student should hold up the appropriate card to indicate whether the word has one, two, or three syllables. Say the word and clap again if needed. Repeat with the remaining items.

Toss 'n Rhyme

Ready: Draw a grid of four squares by five squares on a white shower curtain liner. Write one of the following words in each square: *hat, cat, rat, sat, bed, fed, red, led, big, dig, jig, pig, fog, dog, hog, log, fun, run, sun, bun.* Make sure to randomly distribute the rhyming words when you write them on the mat. Provide two beanbags or make them by stuffing the feet of two socks with dried beans. Tie knots in the tops of the socks.

Set: Place the liner grid on the floor. Divide players into pairs and have them stand around the grid with their partners. Each pair of students will take a turn.

Go: During the turn, each player in the pair should toss her beanbag on a square. Together, they should call out the two words. (If needed, assist them in reading the words.) Then, ask the players if the words rhyme. If they do, the players should give each other a high five, retrieve the beanbags, and pass them to the next pair of players. If the words do not rhyme, the next pair of players should retrieve the beanbags and take a turn.

Count 'n Sort

Ready: Locate stickers or small pictures of items with familiar names, such as a cat, house, car, bird, boy, boat, or tent. The words should not be more than six letters long. Attach each picture to an index card and write the naming word in large letters below the picture. Decorate five shoe boxes and label each with a number from 2-6.

Set: Arrange the cards and shoe boxes on a table.

Go: The player should select a card, say the word, and count the number of letters in the word. Then, she should place the card in the corresponding shoe box and allow the next player to take a turn.

Print Match

Ready: Make environmental print word cards by gluing ads and labels from familiar products and places to index cards. Environmental print words might include names of fast-food restaurants, popular stores, cereals and other food products, toothpastes, or soaps. Make two identical cards for each ad or label.

Set: Shuffle the cards and place them in a box. Select two students to be partners.

Go: Players should take turns selecting word cards, reading them (with help as needed), and placing them on the table. When a player draws a card that has a match already on the table, the first student to say, "Print match!" gets to keep that pair of cards. Play continues until all of the cards have been matched.

Inside and Outside

Ready: Collect pictures showing house interiors and exteriors from home decorating magazines and glue them to construction paper. Consider laminating the pages for durability. Decorate one box with a picture of an interior and label it *inside* and then decorate another box with a picture of an exterior and label it *outside*.

Set: Shuffle the pictures and place them near the two boxes. Select two students to be partners.

Go: Players should take turns selecting pictures and stating either, "This picture is *inside* the house," or "This picture is *outside* the house." Players should place the pictures in the correct boxes.

Roll-A-Rhyme

Ready: Locate a rubber playground ball or beach ball.

Set: Have students sit cross-legged in a large circle.

Go: Say a one-syllable word, such as, "hat," and roll the ball to a student. That student should say a word that rhymes with *hat*. Then, the student should call out a new word and roll the ball to another player. The new player should call out a word that rhymes with the new word. Repeat until all of the players have had turns.

Number Games

Catch a Number

Ready: Inflate enough balloons for each student to have one. With a permanent marker, write a different familiar number, such as 1 through 10, on each balloon. Make a set of matching cards by writing each number on an index card. If, for example, the class includes 20 students but children only know numbers 1 through 10, you can program two balloons for each number and have students perform the activity in pairs. (*Caution:* Before completing any balloon activity, ask parents about possible latex allergies. Also, remember that uninflated or popped balloons may present a choking hazard.)

Set: Put the cards in a small container and place the balloons in a large bag or basket. Have children stand in a large circle. You should stand in the middle of the circle with the balloons and cards.

Go: Select a number card and place it facedown on the floor. Do not let anyone see the number on the card. Call out the name of a student and toss one balloon into the air. That student should move into the center of the circle and catch the balloon. He should return to his place in the circle, still holding the balloon. Continue calling names and tossing balloons. When every child has caught a balloon and returned to the circle, begin slowly counting aloud as a group. When each player hears her number, she should sit on the floor. When everyone is sitting, reveal the number on the card. The child holding that number becomes the leader for the next round. He should collect the balloons, select a new number card, and toss the balloons out again. (If more than one student has the number, they can act as leaders together and take turns tossing balloons.)

Number Teams

Ready: Prepare a variety of game pieces for several familiar numbers, such as 1 through 10. Game pieces for each number could include: an index card with the number written on it, an index card with the number word written on it, an index card with the number of stickers stuck to it, a craft stick with the number of dried beans glued to it, a domino with the total number of dots representing the number, or a playing card representing the number.

Set: Select at least two numbers to use for each round. Gather the game pieces for the numbers you have chosen. Scramble the items and hand them out randomly to students. Each student should receive one game piece.

Go: The object is for students with matching numbers on their game pieces to find each other and form a team. At your signal, players should walk around and compare game pieces with classmates to find their number team. When matches are found, students should sit down together until all of the students have found their teams. If you only selected two numbers for the round, students should eventually sort themselves into two teams; if you selected three numbers, there will be three teams; etc. The first team correctly assembled and seated is the winner. When a team is complete, the rest of the class claps the winning team's number. Collect the game pieces and play again. Add more numbers or switch to new numbers for each round.

"Eye" Spy

Ready: Prepare a number line for each student by writing familiar numbers on a sentence strip. Create an Eye Spy stick for each child by gluing a googly eye to one end of a craft stick. (Or, simply draw a picture of an eye on one end of the stick.) Make a larger number line and Eye Spy stick for yourself.

Set: Seat children at tables or on the floor with their number lines in front of them and Eye Spy sticks in their hands.

Go: Give a clue for a number, such as "I spy the number that is after three." Players should locate the number, point to it with their Eye Spy sticks, and call out, "I spy four!" If necessary, model the process on your number line. Repeat the game with a new clue.

Estimation Game

Ready: Acquire a chalkboard or write-on/wipe-away board for each student, along with writing utensils and clean, old socks or rags to use for erasers. Gather a collection of manipulatives, such as marbles or dried lima beans. You will also need a variety of small jars and containers. (If, for example, children are familiar with numbers through 10, make sure that each container you choose holds no more than 10 manipulatives. You may want to choose larger manipulatives if you are having trouble finding small enough containers.)

Set: Seat children at tables or on the floor with their boards, writing utensils, and erasers.

Go: Display one of the small, empty containers and ask players to estimate how many of a certain manipulative will fit inside it. (Discuss the process of estimating if needed.) Have students write their estimations on their boards. Assist any students who may need help. Then, begin filling the container as you count aloud together. Write the result on the board or chart paper. Ask each child to read his estimate aloud, and have the class call out together, "Too high," "Too low," or "Just right." When all of the students have had a turn to announce their estimates, erase the boards and choose another container. Play again.

How Do You Do?

Ready: Write familiar numbers, such as 1-10, on index cards or sturdy card stock. Make another set of cards with dots that match the numbers.

Set: Give each student one card. Select music that can be easily started and stopped.

Go: Explain that when the music starts, each child should walk around the room until she finds the classmate who has the number or number of dots that matches her card. Then, she should shake hands with her partner and say, "How do you do?" Stop the music when all of the students are matched. Redistribute the cards and play again.

Variation: To practice cooperation skills, tape or safety-pin the cards to the backs of students' shirts. Do not let them see their own cards. Students should walk around the room and help each other find their matches.

Horses

Ready: Gather enough index cards for each student to have one. Write familiar numbers, such as 1-10, on the cards.

Set: Have students stand in a large circle and give each child a card. Tell the children that they are going to pretend to be horses.

Go: To start the game, shout, "Giddyap!" Students should trot around in a circle until you say, "Whoa!" When they come to a stop, call out one of the numbers. All of the players with that number should stomp their "hooves" on the floor the specified number of times. Then, they should trot around the outside of the circle until they get back to their original places. Finally, shout, "Giddyap!" and begin the game again.

Don't Drop the Ball!

Ready: Locate a rubber playground ball.

Set: Have students stand in a large circle and face the middle.

Go: Give the ball to one player and call out a number from 1-10. Have the student pass the ball to the child on her left as the rest of the class counts, "One!" Students should continue passing the ball around the circle and counting aloud each time the ball is caught. Students should start counting again if the ball is dropped. When the designated number is reached, the player should bounce the ball that number of times while the class counts aloud. Then, he should call out a new number and begin passing the ball around the circle again.

Variation: Make the game more difficult by periodically reversing the direction that the ball is traveling.

Copycat ♡ ? ✎

Ready: On index cards, write a variety of simple sound patterns, such as *2 claps, 3 stomps, 2 claps.*

Set: Have students stand in a semicircle. You should stand in front of them so that they can all see you as you demonstrate the pattern. Tell them you will first perform and count a pattern and then they will "copycat" the pattern.

Go: Choose a card from the stack and slowly count aloud while demonstrating the pattern. Then, watch and listen as students repeat it. Demonstrate the pattern a second time if students need extra modeling. Continue the process using the other cards in the stack. Finally, call on players to invent patterns for the class.

Variation: Increase the difficulty by adding other sounds, such as tapping an unsharpened pencil on a desk or making a clicking sound with the tongue.

Bounce 'n Count ♡ ? 〰 👟

Ready: Provide a basketball, rubber playground ball, or beach ball for each student.

Set: Have students stand in a circle and face the middle.

Go: Choose one student to start the game. He should call out a number from 1-10. The other students should then bounce their balls that number of times while counting aloud. The next student in the circle should call out a number. Play continues until all students have had a chance to choose numbers.

Beanbag Predictions

Ready: Provide a beanbag for each student or make beanbags by stuffing the feet of socks with dried beans. Tie knots in the tops of the socks.

Set: Have students stand in a line on the playground or in the gym, all facing the same way, holding their beanbags. Select one player to be the Predictor. She should move slightly away from the class with a pencil and a small notepad. The Predictor should write a number on the notepad to guess how many beanbags will be tossed to the center of the floor.

Go: As a group, say the following chant:

> *Beanbag, beanbag,*
> *Round and round.*
> *How many beanbags*
> *are on the ground?*

Before saying the chant, each student should secretly decide whether to toss his beanbag to the middle of the area or keep it in his hand. Then, as the group says the last word of the chant, the students who have decided to toss their beanbags should simultaneously toss them into the center of the area. The Predictor should go to the center and collect the beanbags as the group counts them aloud. The Predictor should show students the number that she wrote on her notepad. The players should call out, "High!" (Predictor guessed too high), "Low!" (Predictor guessed too low), or "Just right!" (Predictor guessed correctly). Players should collect the beanbags and prepare to play again while you select a new Predictor.

Bowling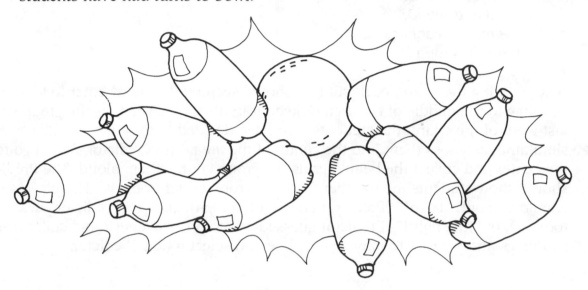

Ready: Gather 10 empty, clean, two-liter bottles and a rubber playground ball. Put a small amount of sand or dried beans in the bottom of each bottle for stability. Close the bottles tightly.

Set: Arrange the "bowling pin" bottles in a triangle on the floor. Place a masking tape line on the floor several feet in front of the "pins."

Go: Have one player stand at the line and roll the ball toward the pins. After his turn, have the class count aloud the number of pins that he knocked down by either counting up from 1 or down from 10. Give the player a clap for each pin he knocked down. Then, reset the bottles for the next student to take a turn. Continue until all students have had turns to bowl.

Which Has the Most?

Ready: Gather a collection of empty baby food jars that are all the same size. Fill each jar with a different item, such as stones, cotton balls, connecting blocks, marbles, dried lima beans, game pieces, or milk caps. Place the tops securely on the jars. Make several copies of the Ballot Patterns (page 47) and cut them apart. You will need enough copies for each student to have one ballot for each round of the game that you play.

Set: Select two of the jars. Label them 1 and 2. Give each student a ballot and a crayon.

Go: Allow players to examine both jars and then "vote" for the jar that they think has the most items inside. Have them mark their selections on their ballots. Next, open the jars and count the items as a class. Reward students who voted correctly with high fives. Repeat the game with two new jars and new ballots.

Ballot Patterns
Activity found on page 46.

Name: _____

☐ **1**   ☐ **2**

Name: _____

☐ **1**   ☐ **2**

Name: _____

☐ **1**   ☐ **2**

CD-104045 *It's Game Time!*

ΛΛΛΛΛΛΛΛΛΛΛΛΛΛΛΛΛΛΛΛΛΛΛΛΛΛΛΛΛΛΛΛΛΛΛΛΛΛΛΛΛ

Hop 'n Count ♡ ? 👟 ....

Ready: Obtain a white shower curtain liner. With a permanent marker, draw a grid of approximately 1' x 1' squares (30.5 cm x 30.5 cm) on the liner and write a different familiar number in each square. Provide a beanbag or make a beanbag by stuffing the foot of a sock with dried beans. Tie a knot in the top of the sock.

Set: Place the grid flat on the floor. Have students stand around the grid.

Go: Each player should take a turn tossing the beanbag on one of the numbered squares on the grid. Then, that player should hop in place that number of times while the other students count aloud.

Variation: Players can perform actions other than hopping, such as clapping, stomping, doing jumping jacks, or giving high fives to classmates.

Gloves and Mittens ♡ 🧤 ....

Ready: Make a child-sized "clothesline" by stretching a piece of yarn between two chairs or sturdy bookcases. Secure the yarn with tape. Collect pairs of gloves and mittens in several sizes, colors, and patterns. Or, make copies of the Gloves and Mittens Patterns (page 49) on a variety of colorful paper or card stock. You may want to draw patterns on the pairs of gloves and mittens to make each pair more distinct. You will also need enough clothespins to hang each glove and mitten.

Set: Mix up the gloves and mittens and place them in a tub near the clothesline. Put the clothespins in a separate container.

Go: Each student should take a turn sorting through the tub to find a matching pair of gloves or mittens and then hang them side-by-side on the clothesline. When all of the gloves and mittens have been sorted and hung on the clothesline, help the class count them aloud. You can count by ones (total number), by twos (total number of pairs), or even by fives (total number of fingers if you only use gloves).

ΛΛΛΛΛΛΛΛΛΛΛΛΛΛΛΛΛΛΛΛΛΛΛΛΛΛΛΛΛΛΛΛΛΛΛΛΛΛΛΛΛ

Gloves and Mittens Patterns

Activity found on page 48.

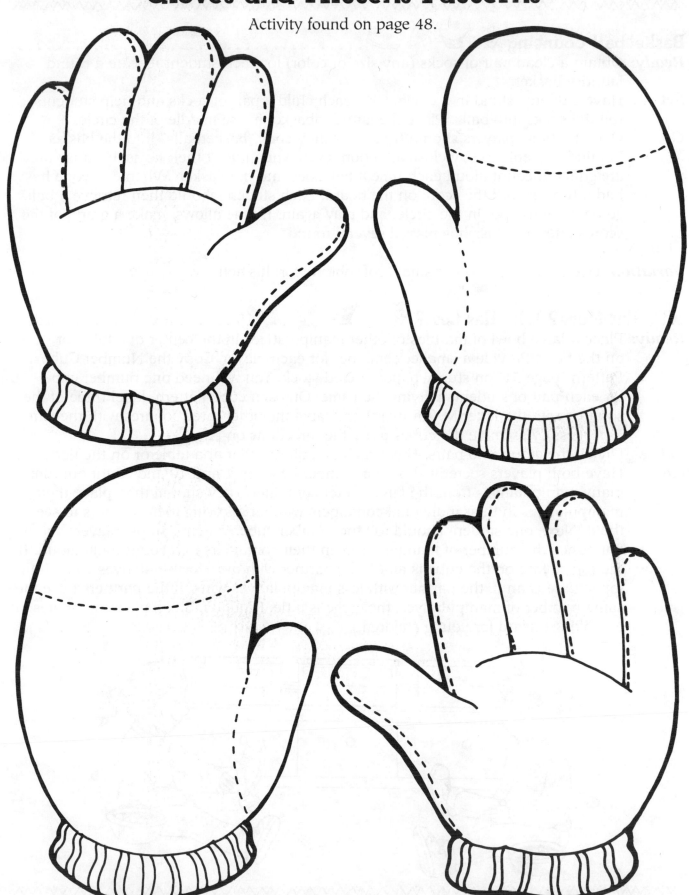

Basketball Counting

Ready: Obtain a clean pair of socks (any size or color) for each student. Locate a round laundry basket.

Set: Have students stand in a circle. Give each child a pair of socks and help students roll the socks into balls. Place the laundry basket in the middle of the circle.

Go: One at a time, players should try to toss their sock "basketballs" into the basket. Remind students to pay close attention, even when it isn't their turns, because they are going to count aloud each time a ball goes into the basket. When everyone has had a turn, record the score on the board. Each student should then retrieve a ball, go back to his spot in the circle, and play again. If time allows, make a graph of the scores after the class has played several rounds.

Variation: Use beanbags or other small, soft objects for this activity.

Who Has More? Who Has Less?

Ready: Place a large bowl of marbles or other manipulatives in the center of a table or on the floor. Provide a smaller container for each player. Copy the Number Cube Pattern (page 51) on sturdy paper or card stock. You will need one number cube for each pair of students playing the game. On each cube pattern, label three of the squares with the letter M (for more) and label the other three squares with the letter L (for less). Assemble the cubes using the directions on page 51.

Set: Divide the group into pairs. Have each pair sit together at a table or on the floor.

Go: Have both players secretly choose a number between 1 and 10 and count out that many manipulatives from the large center container. They should then place their manipulatives in their individual containers without allowing their partners to see them. Next, one student should roll the number cube. When it stops, players should announce the number of manipulatives in their containers and count them aloud. If the top square on the cube is an M, the partner with more manipulatives wins. If the top square is an L, the partner with less manipulatives wins. If the partners have the same number of manipulatives, the game is a tie. (*Caution:* Small pieces may present a choking hazard for young children.)

Number Cube Pattern

Activities found on pages 50, 53, and 54.

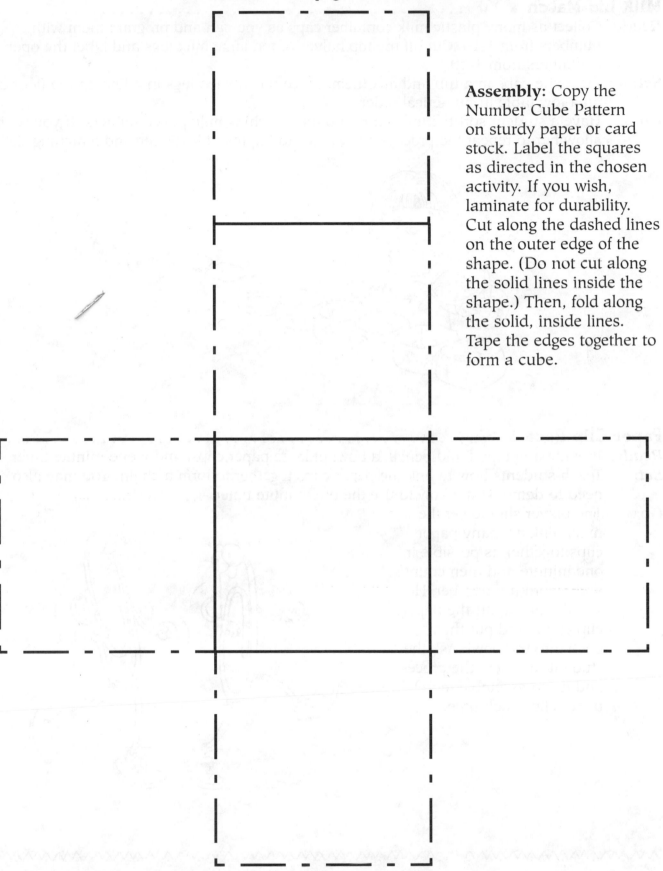

Assembly: Copy the Number Cube Pattern on sturdy paper or card stock. Label the squares as directed in the chosen activity. If you wish, laminate for durability. Cut along the dashed lines on the outer edge of the shape. (Do not cut along the solid lines inside the shape.) Then, fold along the solid, inside lines. Tape the edges together to form a cube.

CD-104045 *It's Game Time!*

Milk Lid Match

Ready: Collect as many plastic milk container caps as you can and program them with numbers from 1-10. Cut off the top halves of ten large milk jugs and label the open containers from 1-10.

Set: Place the caps in a tub and mix them. Place the labeled jugs in a line on the floor or on a low table in numerical order.

Go: Have a student sort the milk caps into the matching milk jug containers. If you wish, allow her to repeat the process a few times to improve identifying and matching skills.

Paper Clip Race

Ready: Provide a notepad and pencil, a bowl of large paper clips, and a one-minute timer.

Set: Teach students how to link the paper clips together to form a chain. You may also need to demonstrate how to use the one-minute timer.

Go: The player should set the timer, link as many paper clips together as possible in one minute and then count and record the number. He should take apart the paper clip chain and put them back into the bowl. Ask the student to repeat the process and try to assemble more paper clips each time.

Rice Predictions

Ready: Fill a large tub with rice. Provide a variety of plastic containers of different shapes and sizes.

Set: Select two students to be partners.

Go: One student should choose a large container and a small container. She should predict how many times the small container will need to be filled and poured to reach the top of the large container. Her partner should count how many times she fills the small container and pours it into the larger container. When the large container is full, the partner should say whether the guess was high, low, or just right. The partners then switch roles.

Road Race

Ready: Make "roads" by taping index cards together end to end, alternating plain white with lined cards or alternating colors so that the cards can be easily counted. Provide one road and a toy car for each child. Copy the Number Cube Pattern (page 51) on sturdy paper or card stock. You will need one number cube for each pair of students playing the game. On each cube pattern, label the squares with different numbers from 1-10. Assemble the cubes using the directions on page 51.

Set: Select two students to be partners. Have partners lay their roads side by side on the floor or a table.

Go: Players take turns rolling the number cube and "driving" their cars over that number of index cards on the road. The first player to reach the end of his road wins. Players then go back to their starting lines and begin again.

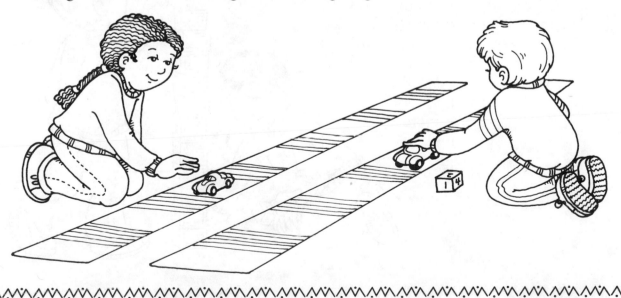

Sticker Check

Ready: Program index cards with familiar numbers. On the back of each card, attach the matching number of stickers. Provide dried beans or manipulatives for counters.

Set: Shuffle the cards and place the stack on the table with the number sides facing up. Place the manipulatives in a small container.

Go: The player should read the number on the top card and then count out that many manipulatives. Next, she should turn over the card and place one manipulative on each sticker to check for one-to-one correspondence. Have the student place the manipulatives back in the bowl and start again with a new card.

Roll 'n Build

Ready: Copy the Number Cube Pattern (page 51) on sturdy paper or card stock. You will need one number cube for each pair of students playing the game. On each cube pattern, label the squares with six different numbers between 1 and 10. Assemble the cubes using the directions on page 51. Provide a set of building blocks.

Set: Clear an area on the floor for students to build a tower.

Go: Players should take turns rolling the number cube and adding that many blocks to a tower. Both players should count aloud as blocks are added to the structure. When the tower falls, the players should begin again with a new tower.

Sticker Match ?

Ready: Make pairs of index cards with matching numbers of stickers on each pair. For example, you will have two cards with one sticker on each card, two cards with two stickers on each card, two cards with three stickers on each card, etc. Use a variety of stickers so that students will match the number of stickers on each card rather than the pictures on the stickers.

Set: Mix up the cards and place them faceup on the floor or table. This game can be played with one or two players.

Go: Instruct each player to locate a matching number pair and arrange them side-by-side. Play continues until all of the pairs are matched. Then, the cards can be reshuffled to play again.

Variation: Place the cards facedown in a grid pattern and have students play a memory matching game. One player should flip over two cards. If they match, he should place them together beside the grid. If they do not match, he should turn them facedown, and the second player should try to find a matching set of cards.

Ring-A-Ling ?

Ready: Acquire a small bell. Collect 10 manipulatives for each student, such as small blocks or dried beans.

Set: Seat students at tables or on the floor with their manipulatives lined in front of them.

Go: Silently select a familiar number. Slowly ring the bell that number of times. Have each student count the rings quietly to herself and then count that number of manipulatives and place them in a separate pile. Finally, ring the bell the same number of times again and have children check their results as you count aloud together. Then, have each student place her manipulatives in a line again and repeat the activity with a new number.

Shape Games

Patterns

Ready: Acquire a sentence strip and a crayon for each student. Select music that can be easily started and stopped.

Set: Seat students in a circle on the floor. Give each child a sentence strip and a crayon. Help him write his name on the back of the strip. Then, instruct students to draw patterns using familiar shapes on the fronts of their strips. The patterns should include three items, such as circle-circle-square or triangle-rectangle-triangle.

Go: Start the music and have players pass the sentence strips around the circle. When the music stops, each student should use her crayon to add the next shape to the pattern she is holding. Continue the game until the sentence strips are filled, then return them to their original owners for checking.

Shape Tallies

Ready: Acquire a chalkboard or write-on/wipe-away board for each student, along with writing utensils and clean, old socks or rags for erasers. On chart paper or the board draw a triangle, circle, square, and rectangle.

Set: Seat students on the floor in front of the board.

Go: Instruct students to secretly select and draw one of the four shapes on their boards. Then, one by one, have players reveal their drawings and call out the shape names as you tally the results on the board. When everyone has had a turn to reveal his choice, count the tallies together and determine which shape wins. Have the children who drew that shape stand and take a bow. Players should erase their boards, choose new shapes to draw, and begin the game again.

Name It ... Make It

Ready: Acquire four craft sticks for each student. Each student will also need an additional craft stick that you have cut in half.

Set: Seat players on the floor near the board or chart paper and distribute the craft sticks.

Go: Draw a familiar shape that can be formed using straight lines, such as a triangle, square, or rectangle. Students should call out the name of the shape and then form it on the floor in front of them using their craft sticks. When everyone is finished, give the shape a cheer, such as "Yeah, squares!" Count the number of sides aloud as children pick up the sticks. Repeat with another shape.

Shake-A-Shape

Ready: Using large, self-stick mailing labels, cut out a set of familiar shapes for each student, such as a circle, rectangle, square, and triangle. Select music that can be easily started and stopped.

Set: Ask players to stick the labels to pieces of their clothing, such as on a shoe, a shirt sleeve, a jeans' leg, or a hat. If you prefer for the class to have the same movements, assign a place to affix each sticker, such as circles on right shoes, squares on left elbows, or rectangles on right shoulders.

Go: Start the music and call out, for example, "Shake your circles." Students should shake the body parts where their circle stickers are affixed until the music stops. Restart the music and play again with another shape.

Put It There

Ready: Prepare two different cardboard shapes for each student, such as a circle and a square. You can also use laminated, sturdy card stock.

Set: Have students stand in a circle and give each child two shapes, one for each hand.

Go: Call out instructions, such as "Put the square on your right shoulder," "Put the circle under your chin," "Put the circle on your left knee," "Put the square on your nose," etc. When children become more adept, allow them to take turns calling out directions.

Shape Hunt

Ready: Prepare several construction paper shapes of different colors and sizes. You may want to laminate the shapes for durability. Create a container for each shape by attaching a paper shape to the front of each container. Line the containers on a table at the front of the room. Select music that can be easily started and stopped.

Set: Hide the shapes throughout the classroom.

Go: Select one shape container, show it to students, and have them name the shape that is on the front. Tell them that while the music is playing, they are going to look for only that paper shape in the classroom. Explain that the paper may be another color or another size, but it should be the same shape. Start the music and allow time for children to find all or most of the shapes. When the music stops, players should put their shapes in the container. Select another shape to begin the game again.

Shape Walk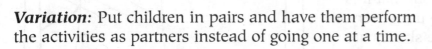

Ready: Draw and cut out large, familiar shapes, such as a circle, square, triangle, and rectangle, using butcher paper or poster board. Consider laminating the shapes for durability.

Set: Tape the shapes to the floor randomly throughout the room. Gather students in a line against one wall.

Go: Chant the following poem to each child:

> *I see a (circle). Please (walk) to it.*
> *Now, (walk) around it. I know you can do it!*

For each child, say a different shape and a different action, such as walk, run, jog, trot, march, gallop, skip, or hop. The child performing the action should follow the outline of the shape when she is going around it.

Variation: Put children in pairs and have them perform the activities as partners instead of going one at a time.

Pasta Match

Ready: Collect several different shapes of dried pasta. Glue one of each to a clothespin.

Set: Mix the remaining pasta in a large plastic container or bag. Clip each clothespin to a separate small plastic container.

Go: Students should sort the pasta from the large container or bag into the appropriate small containers. If you wish, challenge them to try to work faster as they master the sorting process.

Shape Match

Ready: Prepare a variety of familiar shapes—circles, squares, rectangles, triangles, etc.—using construction paper. Make several copies of each shape. You may want to laminate the shapes for durability. Be sure that each shape you choose is represented several times in the classroom setting.

Set: Attach non-permanent adhesive to the backs of the shapes and display them on a table.

Go: One player should select a paper shape, find an object in the room where that shape is represented, and affix it to the matching object. For example, a player might attach a rectangle to a rectangular table, a circle to a round clock, or a square to a square window. The child should then give a high five to the next student in the group to signal that it is her turn. Continue playing until everyone has had a turn or all of the shapes are matched. Collect the shapes from around the room and play again.

Making Squares Mini-Book

Ready: Copy the Mini-Book Pattern (pages 61-62). Be sure to copy the pattern double sided as it appears on pages 61-62. You will need enough copies for each pair of students to have one mini-book to share. To assemble a mini-book: Cut along the dashed border lines to remove the page title and number. Cut the page in half along the horizontal, dashed line. Put the pages in order and staple twice along the solid line. Fold the book in half vertically along the solid line.

Set: Select two students to be partners.

Go: Have partners read the mini-book together and then play the game using the grid on page 8 of the mini-book. If you wish, recreate the grid on page 8 and make several copies so that students can play the Making Squares game again.

Mini-Book Pattern

Activity found on page 60.

I will draw a line. 4

I made a square. 5

Let's play a game. 2

You won, Kim! 7

Mini-Book Pattern

Activity found on page 60.

I made a square, too. 6

You draw a line. 3

Making Squares

You can play, too! 8

1

〰〰〰〰〰〰〰〰〰〰〰〰〰〰〰〰〰〰〰〰〰〰〰〰〰〰

Circle Clues 🖤 ❓ 〰 🖐 ....

Ready: On index cards, write the names of several round objects, such as a clock, pizza, coin, smiley face, pie, balloon, sun, ball, bead, bubble, full moon, and tire. Acquire a large sheet of butcher paper or several sheets of chart paper.

Set: Put the paper on a table or on the floor and arrange students around it. Provide a marker or crayon for the team. You might choose to have several teams play at once, in which case you should provide paper and a marker for each team.

Go: Give the marker to one player on the team. Select an index card and give a clue about the word, such as, "It's round, and it shows us when it is time for recess." The players should confer to try to guess the object. If students are having trouble guessing the object, give another clue, such as, "It has numbers on it." When players think they know what the item is, the player with the marker should draw the team's guess on the paper. Then, the team should announce their guess, for example, "It's a clock!" If they are correct, students should give themselves a "round" of applause by clapping their hands in a circle shape in the air. Then, the next player on the team should take the marker while you select another index card to play again.

Jump Rope Shapes ❓ 🖐 👟 ....

Ready: Collect enough jump ropes for each child to have one.

Set: Spread students around the play area with plenty of space between children. Give each child a jump rope.

Go: Call out the name of a familiar shape. Players should arrange their jump ropes on the ground in that shape. As each student finishes forming the outline of the shape, check his work and assist as needed. When all of the students have formed the shape successfully, call out, "Good for you! Now, jump through!" Each student should jump inside the shape, give himself a pat on the back, and applaud. Then, have students pick up the jump ropes and wait for the next shape instruction.

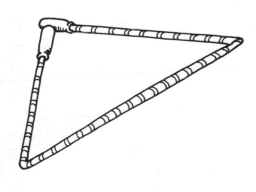

〰〰〰〰〰〰〰〰〰〰〰〰〰〰〰〰〰〰〰〰〰〰〰〰〰〰

Time Games

Before and After

Ready: Collect a variety of pictures of items from magazines, such as a car, cat, and hairbrush. Glue the pictures to sturdy paper. You may want to use a variety of small objects instead of pictures.

Set: Divide students into pairs and give each pair a picture or an object.

Go: Give each pair a few minutes to plan their "before" and "after" scenarios, then have them sit down to indicate that they are ready to play. Once all of the pairs are seated, begin calling on pairs one at a time. As you call on each pair, the players should stand. One child should tell a "before" action related to the picture or object and the second child should tell an "after" action. Encourage them to use complete sentences. For example, if a pair were given a picture of a toy car, the first player might say, "*Before* I ride in the car, I fasten my seat belt." The second player might say, "*After* I ride in the car, I visit my grandmother."

Now and Then

Ready: Collect a variety of pictures of people, toys, modes of transportation, houses, and memorabilia from long ago, as well as pictures of similar items from modern times. Consider searching magazines, encyclopedias, and Internet sources to find pictures. Glue pictures to sturdy card stock and laminate for durability.

Set: Shuffle the pictures. Discuss the terms *now* and *then* with students.

Go: Hold up a picture. Students should decide if they think the picture is from long ago (then) or from modern times (now) and call out, "Now!" or "Then!" accordingly. Discuss opinions about the picture. Ask students what gave them clues to decide if the picture was old or new. Continue showing pictures and having students guess the time periods.

/\

First, Next, Then ♡ ? ◡ ....

Ready: Program index cards with the names of topics or procedures that can be described in at least three steps, such as cleaning your room, making a sandwich, the life cycle of a butterfly, a day at school, or feeding a pet. Add a picture clue to each card using a matching sticker or a simple illustration.

Set: Divide students into teams of three. Give each team a card and help them read and understand the topic. Make sure that only the team members hear the topic—other teams will try to guess the topic later in the game.

Go: Give teams time to plan, then have them sit down together to indicate that they are ready to play. Once all teams are seated, select a team to begin the game. Each player on the team should present a step to describe their topic or procedure using the sequencing words *first*, *next*, and *then*. The rest of the class should try to guess the topic or procedure that is written on the index card. For example, if a team is given the "cleaning your room" card, the first player might say, "*First*, you pick up your toys." Player two might say, "*Next*, you make your bed," and player three might add, "*Then*, you sweep the floor." The class would guess that the procedure is cleaning your room.

Days-of-the-Week Towers ? ◡ ◔ ....

Ready: Write the days of the week on index cards. Collect seven blocks for each student and for yourself. Write the days of the week in order across the board and number them from one to seven.

Set: Have children sit at tables or on the floor with their blocks in front of them. Sit with them with your own blocks in front of you.

Go: Select a card from the stack and say, for example, "Let's build a Friday tower." Together, say the names of the days of the week in order. Stack a block for each day and stop when you reach Friday. Then, using the numbers and words on the board as a reference, count the blocks aloud together to make sure you have the correct number of blocks in the stack. (For Friday, there should be five blocks in the tower if you choose to start the sequence with Monday. If you start with Sunday, a Friday tower would have six blocks.) Take down the towers, select a new card, and play again.

/\

ΛΛ∿ΛΛ∿ΛΛ∿ΛΛ∿ΛΛ∿ΛΛ∿ΛΛ∿ΛΛ∿ΛΛ∿ΛΛ∿ΛΛ∿ΛΛ∿ΛΛ∿ΛΛ∿

Day or Night?

Ready: Cut out a large sun and a large moon from sheets of construction paper. Post them on opposite sides of the room.

Set: Seat students on the floor in the middle of the room. Discuss a variety of activities that occur during the daytime as you stand by the picture of the sun and discuss nighttime activities as you stand by the picture of the moon.

Go: Call out an activity, such as eating breakfast, and ask students to decide if the activity is a daytime or nighttime activity. Ask them to stand by the sun or the moon to symbolize their decisions. Other activities to consider calling out might be playing outside, dreaming, going to recess, or reading a bedtime story. Players' opinions might differ about some times, such as taking a bath, and they may do some activities both day and night, such as watching cartoons or brushing teeth. In this case, have them stand in the middle of the room and point to both symbols. When opinions differ, discuss why and talk about how some people do things at different times.

Night, Night, Day

Ready: Write each student's name on a craft stick and place the sticks in an empty jar.

Set: Select a stick from the jar. The student whose name is on the stick gets to be the Dream Chaser first. Have the rest of the class sit on the floor in a large circle.

Go: Explain that "Night, Night, Day" is a variation of "Duck, Duck, Goose." The students in the circle should close their eyes and pretend to be asleep. The Dream Chaser should walk around the outside of the circle, gently tapping each player's head, and saying, "Night." When the Dream Chaser decides to say, "Day!" instead of "Night," the child who is tapped should "wake up" and chase the Dream Chaser around the circle. If the Dream Chaser is able to run all the way around the circle and sit in the empty space before the chosen student catches her, then she is safe and the other student becomes the new Dream Chaser. If the Dream Chaser is tagged before she can reach the empty space, then she should sit in the middle of the circle for one round while the other student becomes the Dream Chaser. She can rejoin the circle for the next round.

ΛΛ∿ΛΛ∿ΛΛ∿ΛΛ∿ΛΛ∿ΛΛ∿ΛΛ∿ΛΛ∿ΛΛ∿ΛΛ∿ΛΛ∿ΛΛ∿ΛΛ∿ΛΛ∿

What Time Is It?

Ready: Make two copies of the Blank Clock Cards (page 68). Program each clock to a different hourly time, from 1:00 to 12:00. Cut apart the cards and laminate for durability.

Set: Choose one child to be the Timekeeper and stand at one end of the play area. The other students should line up side-by-side at the opposite end of the play area, facing the Timekeeper. Shuffle the clock cards and place them facedown near the Timekeeper.

Go: The players should call out, "What time is it?" The Timekeeper should select a clock from the stack, read it, and shout, "It's (four) o'clock!" (filling in the correct time). The rest of the students should take that many steps toward the Timekeeper, counting aloud in unison.

(For example, if the time is four o'clock, the group would chant, "One o'clock, two o'clock, three o'clock, four o'clock!" while taking four steps.) The process is repeated until the players reach the Timekeeper. When they reach him, the group returns to the starting line, another Timekeeper is chosen, the clocks are reshuffled, and the game begins again.

Days of the Week

Ready: Write students' names on craft sticks and place them in an empty jar or can.

Set: Have players stand in a large circle.

Go: Choose a stick from the jar and call out the name. That student should walk around the outside of the circle and gently touch players' backs one at a time as the class chants, "Sunday, Monday, Tuesday, Wednesday, Thursday, Friday, *Saturday!*" The child who is patted on the word "Saturday" should move out of the circle and sit to the side. The player who was tapping students should take the empty place in the circle. Now, choose another stick and call out the name. That player becomes the next student to walk around the circle and pat players who are still standing. Continue until there are only two players left standing, at which time you become "it." Walk around the two-student circle tapping each one on the back as the class chants the days of the week. Once the winner is determined, everyone may rejoin the circle and begin again.

Variation: For a challenge, use the names of the months instead of days of the week.

Blank Clock Cards

Activities found on pages 5, 6, 9, 11, 67, and 69.

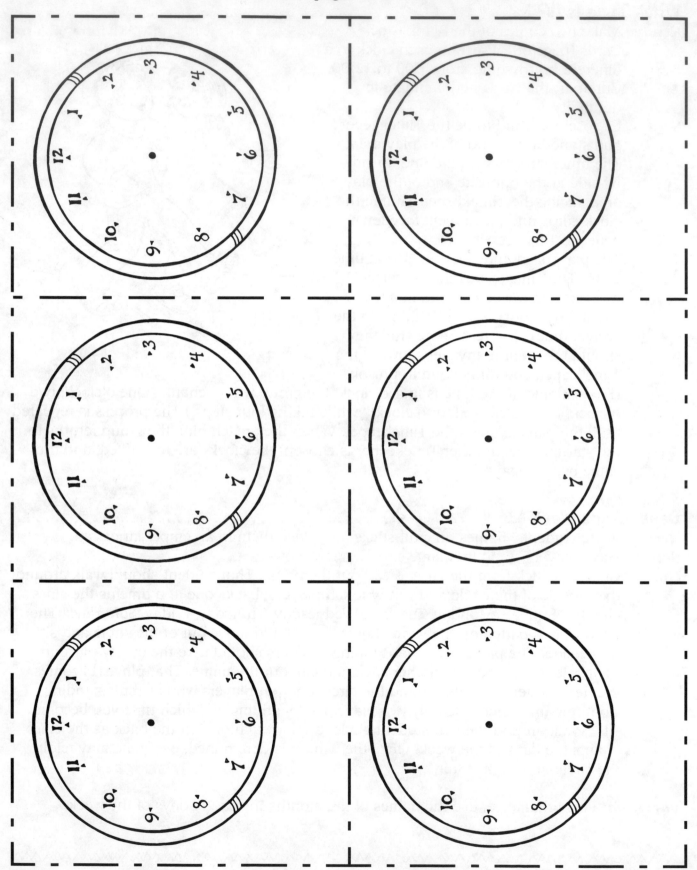

CD-104045 *It's Game Time!*

ΛΛΛΛΛΛΛΛΛΛΛΛΛΛΛΛΛΛΛΛΛΛΛΛΛΛΛΛΛΛΛΛΛΛ

Sock O'Clock 💗 ? 👖 👟 . . . .

Ready: Draw a large clock face on a white shower curtain liner. Draw the minute hand ("big hand") pointing to the 12. On index cards, write hourly times from 1:00 to 12:00.

Set: Lay the clock mat on the floor. Have students take off their shoes and sit on the floor around the mat.

Go: The first player should secretly draw a card and then become the hour hand ("little hand") by sitting on the center dot and pointing to the appropriate hour number with his sock feet. The other children should then call out the time that is being represented. Continue playing until each child has a chance to be the hour hand.

Variation: If you wish to provide a visual aid, make two copies of the Blank Clock Cards (page 68). On the cards, draw the hands to represent hourly times from 1:00 to 12:00 and write the times in digital format below the clocks. Laminate the cards for durability. When students use these cards, they can consult the analog images to help them know where to point their feet.

Time Match 💗 ? 👖 ✊ . . . .

Ready: Prepare individual clocks by copying the Blank Clock Pattern (page 70) on sturdy paper or card stock. Cut and glue the clock faces to paper plates. Attach the clock hands to the center of the paper plates using paper fasteners. Make two copies of the Blank Clock Cards (page 68). On the cards, draw the hands to represent hourly times from 1:00 to 12:00 and write the times in digital format below the clocks. Laminate the cards for durability.

Set: Place the paper plate clocks on a table. Shuffle the time cards and put them facedown on the table. Select two students to be partners.

Go: One partner should select a card and read the time while the other partner sets the time on the paper plate clock. When both partners agree that the time is correct, they should call out, "Ticktock! (Six) o'clock!" Have players switch roles and play the game again.

Variation: If students are comfortable recognizing numbers 1 through 12, write the hourly times in digital format on index cards. Do not provide the analog drawings. Use these cards in place of the clock cards from page 68.

ΛΛΛΛΛΛΛΛΛΛΛΛΛΛΛΛΛΛΛΛΛΛΛΛΛΛΛΛΛΛΛΛΛΛ

Blank Clock Pattern

Activity found on page 69.

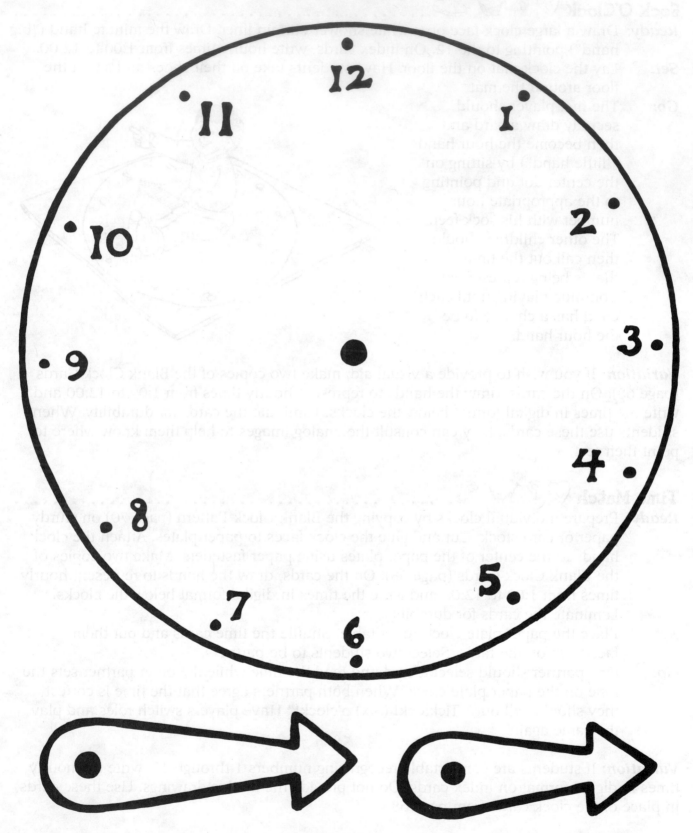

〜〜〜〜〜〜〜〜〜〜〜〜〜〜〜〜〜〜〜〜〜〜〜〜〜〜〜〜〜〜

Spring, Summer, Winter, Fall  . . . .

Ready: Make copies of the Seasonal Trees (pages 72-73). Enlarge the trees and mount each one on a piece of poster board. Color the trees using appropriate seasonal colors. Hang them in the four corners of the room.

Set: Have students gather together in the center of the room. Select one student to be the Season Selector.

Go: Instruct the Season Selector to cover her eyes and chant, "Spring, summer, winter, fall, choose your favorite on the wall!" The remaining students should quietly scramble to stand by one of the four season posters. With her eyes still covered, the Season Selector should call out one of the season names. All of the players standing by that poster must return to the center of the room and be seated. Choose a new Season Selector from the students who are still standing while the selector from the previous round goes to stand at one of the season posters. The new Season Selector should cover his eyes and say the chant while the remaining students either stay where they are or quietly move to other corners. When four or fewer children are left, each must select a different corner. The game ends when only one child is left. This child will be the first Season Selector for the next game.

〜〜〜〜〜〜〜〜〜〜〜〜〜〜〜〜〜〜〜〜〜〜〜〜〜〜〜〜〜〜

Seasonal Trees

Activity found on page 71.

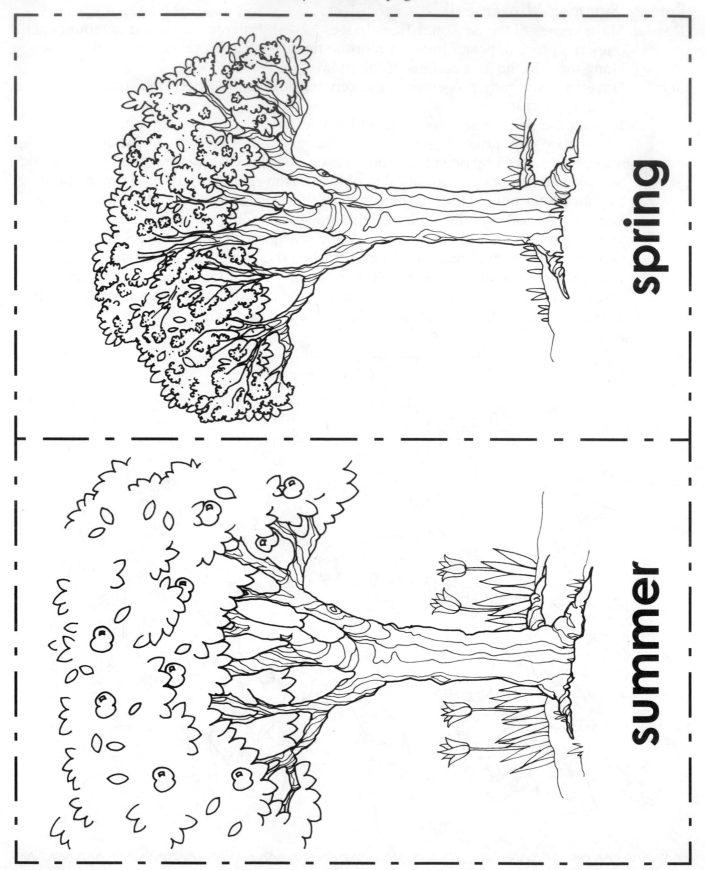

spring

summer

Seasonal Trees

Activity found on page 71.

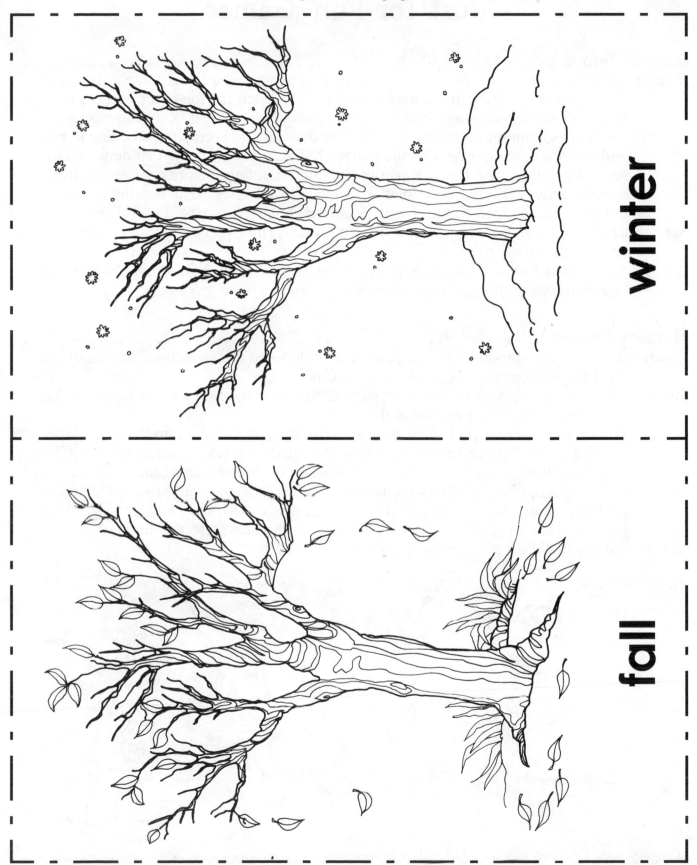

winter

fall

73

"Just for Fun" Games

Balloon Tennis

Ready: To make a simple "tennis racket," stretch and bend a wire hanger into a diamond shape. Bend the hook into a loop for a handle. Stretch the toe of a clean nylon stocking over the diamond-end of the hanger and pull it tight. Knot the stocking where the diamond meets the handle. Use duct tape to secure the stocking in place and cover any sharp edges on the hanger. Make a racket for each student. Inflate several balloons, one for each pair of students. (*Caution:* Before completing any balloon activity, ask parents about possible latex allergies. Also, remember that uninflated or popped balloons may present a choking hazard.)

Set: Clear a large space or go outside if it isn't windy. Have players stand a short distance apart, facing their partners.

Go: As students hit the balloons back and forth to each other, have them count aloud how many times they can hit them before they touch the ground.

Mystery Leader

Ready: Have players stand in a circle. Select one child to be the Detective. She should wait outside the room until you ask her to return.

Set: Select another player to be the Mystery Leader. Ask the Detective to return to the room and stand in the middle of the circle.

Go: The Mystery Leader should model an action, such as hopping, nodding, or clapping, and the other children in the circle should immediately do the same action while counting aloud to 10. When the group reaches 10, the Mystery Leader should begin a new action, and the others should mimic it, again to the count of 10. This process continues until the Detective is able to guess who the Mystery Leader is. When she guesses correctly, the Mystery Leader becomes the new Detective and goes outside the room while a new leader is chosen.

Look What We Can Do!

Ready: Have students stand in a line and count off by fours. The four groups should gather in four sections of the play area.

Set: Each group should secretly select a movement to perform, such as hopping, skipping, twirling, or touching their toes.

Go: One at a time, each group should perform their movement while saying, "Look what we can do! Can you do it, too?" The other groups should join in the activity. Continue until each group has had the opportunity to perform.

Freeze!

Ready: Select upbeat music that can easily be started and stopped.

Set: Have students scatter around the room.

Go: Start the music and encourage players to dance or move in any way that they choose. When the music stops, they should immediately "freeze" in whatever positions they are in and try to keep their balance until the music begins again. If you catch them moving while the music is stopped, they should sit down in their places. Continue until there is only one student left standing, then have everyone stand up to play again.

Beanbag Squeeze

Ready: Provide a large beanbag for each pair of students or make beanbags by stuffing the feet of socks with dried beans. Tie knots in the tops of the socks.

Set: Have each student stand with a partner. Give each pair a beanbag.

Go: Call out an instruction, such as, "Squeeze the beanbag between your backs." The partners should stand back to back with the beanbag between their backs, squeeze together, and hold the beanbag in place as they count to 10. Or, instruct students to squeeze the beanbag between their arms, shoulders, knees, shoes, pinkies, or elbows.

You 'n Me

Ready: Collect old newspapers and tear them into individual pages. You will need enough pages for each pair of students to have three pages. Collect enough rulers for each student to have one. Mark a start and finish line on opposite sides of the room.

Set: Divide students into pairs. Each pair should crumple their newspaper pages into three balls and put them in a row on the start line in front of them. Give each child a ruler.

Go: At your signal, each pair of players should pick up one newspaper ball by holding it between their two rulers. Students should not touch the newspaper ball with their hands during this activity. Once they lift the ball off the ground, they should carry it as quickly as possible to the finish line and put it on the ground. If the ball is dropped, the partners should pick it up without using their hands and keep going. From the finish line, the partners should run back to the start line, pick up another paper ball, and go again. Repeat the process until all of the paper balls have been carried across the finish line.

Meet Me in the Middle

Ready: On index cards, write ways that students can move forward, such as *march*, *jog*, *walk*, *run*, *gallop*, *duck walk*, *skip*, *jump*, *hop*, *crawl*, *"fly,"* *crab walk*, and *trot*.

Set: Divide students into pairs. Partners should stand facing each other at opposite ends of a large, clear play area.

Go: Select one of the cards and call out the action. Then, say, "Meet me in the middle!" Players should perform the action while moving toward their partners. As soon as they meet, they should give each other a high five and sit down. The first team to sit down is the winner for the round.

Mirror

Ready: Bring a mirror to class. Have students take turns looking at the mirror as you discuss the word "reflection."

Set: Divide the class into pairs and have each set of partners stand facing each other. Have them decide who is going to be reflected first and who will be the "mirror."

Go: The player who is being reflected should make very deliberate, slow movements, and the mirror should "reflect" what the first player is doing. After a few minutes, have players switch roles.

Recall

Ready: Select a box that has a flap lid, such as a school supply box. Locate a number of small items that will fit inside the box, such as a yo-yo, magnetic letter, pair of child's sunglasses, bandage, spoon, comb, and baby rattle.

Set: Select two students to be partners.

Go: One player should secretly choose 3-5 items to put inside the box. She should then lift the lid, show her partner the items inside while counting to five, and close the lid. Then, the second player should try to name the items that he saw inside the box. If he is correct, the two players should switch roles. If he is not able to name all of the items correctly on the first try, the first player should show him the contents one more time so that he can guess again.

Index of Activities by Skill

∧∨∧∨∧∨∧∨∧∨∧∨∧∨∧∨∧∨∧∨∧∨∧∨∧∨∧∨∧∨∧∨∧∨∧∨∧∨∧

Oral Language Skills

∧∨∧∨∧∨∧∨∧∨∧∨∧∨∧∨∧∨∧∨∧∨∧∨∧∨∧∨∧∨∧∨∧∨∧∨∧∨∧

Index of Activities by Skill

ᐱᐱ

ᐱᐱ